NEVER

EVER

GIVE UP

SUSANNE STARCK

Great Quotations

Glendale Heights, IL 60139

Compiled by Susanne Starck

Cover Design by Design Dynamics
Typeset Design by Julie Otlewis

Published by Great Quotations, Inc.

Library of Congress Catalog Card Number : 98-075795

ISBN: 1-56245-371-8

Printed in Hong Kong

This book is dedicated with love

and admiration to my father.

Never give up!

—New Testament

Victory has a thousand fathers,
but defeat is an orphan.

— John F. Kennedy

Great works are performed not
by strength, but by perseverance.

— Samuel Johnson

The idea in this game isn't to win popularity polls or to be a good guy to everyone. The name of the game is win.

— Billy Martin

Once you hear the details of a victory it's hard to distinguish it from a defeat.

— Jean-Paul Sarte

You need to realize that whatever it is you want of life, it is there for the taking.

— Robert Collies

Nobody remembers who came
in second.

— Charles Schulz

In a negotiation, he who
cares less, wins.

— Anonymous

Success is not so much
achievement as achieving.
Refuse to join the cautious crowd
that plays not to lose;
play to win.

— David J. Mahoney

The secret to keeping winning streaks going is to maximize the victories while at the same time minimizing the defeats.

— John Lowenstein

Those who tell you it's tough at the top have never been at the bottom.

— Joe Harvey

Within you right now is the power to do things you never dreamed possible. This power becomes available to you just as soon as you can change your beliefs.

— Maxwell Maltz

If an individual wants to be a leader and he isn't controversial that means he hasn't stood for anything.

— Richard M. Nixon

The difference between perseverance and obstinacy is that one comes from a strong will, and the other from a strong won't.

— Henry Ward Beecher

Diamonds are only chunks of
coal, that stuck to their jobs,
you see.

— Minnie Richard Smith

You're never too bad to win.

— Tom McElligott

The most important thing in the Olympic Games is not winning but taking part. The essential thing in life is not conquering but fighting well.

— Baron Pierre de Coubertin

It's a silly game where
nobody wins.

— Thomas Fuller

Hit the ball over the fence and
you can take your time going
around the bases.

— John W. Raper

He who would leap high must
take a long run.

— Danish Proverb

To follow, without hold, one aim:
That's the secret of success.

— Anna Pavlova

When the sun is shining I can do anything; no mountain is too high, no trouble too difficult to overcome.

— Wilma Rudolph

Just don't give up trying to do
what you really want to do.
Where there's love and inspiration,
I don't think you can go wrong.

— Ella Fitzgerald

Oh, we all get run over once in our lives. But one must pick oneself up again. And behave as if it were nothing.

— Henrik Ibsen

The only place winning comes before work is in the dictionary.

First say to yourself what you would be; and then do what you have to do.

— Epictetus

Our doubts are traitors, And make us lose the good we oft might win, by fearing to attempt.

— William Shakespeare

All great achievements
require time.

— David Joseph Schwartz

The greatest mistake a man
can make is to be afraid
of making one.

— Elbert Hubbard

You have to pay the price -
but if you do you can only win.

— Frank Leahy

Victory -
a matter of staying power.

— Elbert Hubbard

Tragedy is a tool for the living to gain wisdom, not a guide by which to live.

— Robert F. Kennedy

Every time you win you're reborn; when you lose, you die a little.

— George Allen

There is no such thing as
no chance.

— Henry Ford

Winning isn't everything.
It's the only thing.

— Vince Lombardi

I want this team to win,
I'm obsessed with winning,
with discipline, with achieving.
That's what this country's
all about.

— George Steinbrenner

Show me a good and gracious loser,
and I'll show you a failure.

— Knute Rockne

No one knows what he can do till
he tries.

— Publilius Syrus

To finish first you must
first finish.

— Rick Mears

You have to learn the rules of the game. And then you have to play better than anyone else.

— Dianne Feinstein

All our dreams can come true, if we have the desire to pursue them.

— Walt Disney

You just keep pushing.
You just keep pushing.
I made every mistake that
could be made.
But I just kept pushing.

— Rene McPherson

Don't fall before you're pushed.

— English Proverb

Those who live are those
who fight.

— Victor Hugo

When things get rough,
remember it's the rubbing that
brings out the shine.

If you can't win, make the fellow
ahead of you break the record.

— Anonymous

Fall seven times, stand up eight.

— Japanese Proverb

In sports you simply aren't considered a real champion until you have defended your title successfully. Winning it once can be a fluke; winning it twice proves you are the best.

— Althea Gibson

We all have possibilities we don't know about. We can do things we don't even dream we can do.

— Dale Carnegie

The only lack or limitation is in your own mind.

— N. H. Moos

I know winning, I'm a winner,
winning is inside me.

— Margaret Avery

In business, the competition will
bite you if you keep running;
if you stand still, they will
swallow you.

— William Knudsen, Jr.

You may be disappointed if you
fail, but you are doomed if you
don't try.

— Beverly Sills

The first principle of success
is desire - knowing what you
want. Desire is the planting
of your seed.

— Robert Collier

We make way for the man who
boldly pushes past us.

— Christian Nestell Bovee

When you come to the end of
your rope, tie a knot and hang on.

— Franklin D. Roosevelt

Big shots are only little shots
who keep shooting.

— Christopher Morley

Whatever you are by nature, keep to it; never desert your line of talent. Be what nature intended you for and you will succeed.

— Sydney Smith

My experience has been . . .
that in the end, when you fight
for a desperate cause and have
good reasons to fight,
you usually win.

— Edward Teller

If you would convince others,
seem open to conviction yourself.

— Lord Chesterfield

The thing that contributes to
anyone reaching the goal he
wants is simply wanting that
goal badly enough.

— Charles E. Wilson

A competitive world has two
possibilities for you. You can lose.
Or, if you want to win,
you can change.

— Lester C. Thurow

If you think you can win,
you can win.
Faith is necessary to victory.

— William Hazlitt

There is always room at the top.

— Daniel Webster

The will to win is important,
but the will to prepare is vital.

— Joe Paterno

When you win nothing hurts.

— Joe Namath

Victory puts us on a level
with heaven.

— Lucretius

Regardless of who you are or
what you have been, you can be
what you want to be.

— W. Clement Stone

You're a hero when you win
and a bum when you lose.
That's the game.

— Johnny Unitas

If your determination is fixed,
I do not counsel you to despair.
Few things are impossible to
diligence and skill. Great works
are performed not by strength
but perseverance.

— Samuel Johnson

I play to win, whether during practice or a real game. And I will not let anything get in the way of me and my competitive enthusiasm to win.

— Michael Jordan

Don't let your will roar when
your power only whispers.

— Thomas Fuller

Do what you can, with what you
have, where you are.

— Theodore Roosevelt

The best index to a person's character is how he treats people who can't do him any good, and how he treats people who can't fight back.

— Abigail Van Buren

When written in Chinese, the word crisis is composed of two characters. One represents danger and the other represents opportunity.

— John F. Kennedy

Winning the Nobel Prize in physics wasn't half as exciting as doing the work itself.

— Maria Goeppert Mayer

Victory often changes her side.

— Homer

Always imitate the behavior of
the winners when you lose.

— Anonymous

You have to already have
convinced yourself that you are
going to win no matter what the
other influences are.

— Edwin Moses

Make no little plans; they have no magic to stir men's blood... Make big plans, aim high in hope and work.

— Daniel H. Burnham

Determination and perseverance move the world; thinking that others will do it for you is a sure way to fail.

— Marva Collins

You win some, you lose some,
and some get rained out, but you
gotta suit up for them all.

— J. Askenberg

There is no finish line.

— Nike Corporation motto

Be there a will, and wisdom
finds a way.

— George Crabbe

The thing to try when all else
fails is: again.

Aim at the sun, and you may not
reach it; but your arrow will fly
higher than aimed at an object on
a level with yourself.

— Joel Hawes

There is in this world no such force as the force of a man determined to rise.

— W. E. B. Du Bois

We will either find a way or make one.

— Hannibal

You learn that, whatever you are doing in life, obstacles don't matter very much. Pain or other circumstances can be there, but if you want to do a job bad enough, you'll find a way to get it done.

— Jack Youngblood

Don't get hung up on a snag in the stream, my dear. Snags alone are not so dangerous - it's the debris that clings to them that makes the trouble. Pull yourself loose and go on.

— Anne Shannon Monroe

Lose as if you like it; win as if you were used to it.

— Tommy Hitchcock

There are no gains without pains.

— Adlai Stevenson

Whoever said, "It's not whether
you win or lose that counts,"
probably lost.

— Martina Navratilova

For when the Great Scorer comes
to mark against your name,
He writes not if you win or lose
but how you played the game.

— Grantland Rice

Never give in, never, never never -
in nothing great or small, large or
petty - never give in - except in
convictions of honor and
good sense.

— Tom Bradley

It isn't the mountain ahead that wears you out - it's the grain of sand in your shoe.

— Robert Service

Mind is all that counts. You can be whatever you make up your mind to be.

— Robert Collier

It is the race or individual that exercises the most patience, forbearance, and self-control in the midst of trying conditions that wins.

— Booker T. Washington

It is only when you despair of all ordinary means, it is only when you convince it that it must help you or you perish, that the seed of life in you stirs itself to provide a new resource.

— Robert Collier

Luck is what happens when preparation meets opportunity.

— Darel Royal

One shining quality lends a lustre to another, or hides some glaring defect.

— William Hazlitt

Anybody can win, unless there happens to be a second entry.

— George Ade

It is only by doing things that one learns how to do things.

— E. W. Scripps

When you reach for the stars,
you may not quite get one,
but you won't come up with a
handful of mud either.

— Leo Burnett

In life, as in a football game,
the principle to follow is:
Hit the hard line.

— Theodore Roosevelt

At any one moment, we have
more possibilities than we have
ability to act upon.

You have to know you can win.
You have to think you can win.
You have to feel you can win.

— Sugar Ray Leonard

Make up your mind to act decidedly and take the consequences. No good is ever done in this world by hesitation.

— Thomas Henry Huxley

We can achieve nothing without
paying the price.

— Earl Nightingale

Start from the bottom up and
work like a son of a gun.

— Fats Waller

Boys, there ain't no free lunches in this country. And don't go spending your whole life commiserating that you got the raw deals. You've got to say, "I think that if I keep working at this and want it bad enough I can have it." It's called perseverance.

— Lee Iacocca

Here's one thing I've said many times to the people I've encouraged along and I hope you will remember it. If you want to make it, you can. You can move up the level system. You can become confident in yourself. You can graduate, if you want to.

— Annabel Victoria Safire

I can give you a six-word formula for success: Think things through - then follow through.

— Eddie Rickenbacker

The achievement of your goal is assured the moment you commit yourself to it.

— Mack R. Douglas

Other Titles by Great Quotations, Inc.

Hard Covers

Ancient Echoes
Behold the Golfer
Commanders in Chief
The Essence of Music
First Ladies
Good Lies for Ladies
Great Quotes From Great Teachers
Great Women
I Thought of You Today
Journey to Success
Just Between Friends
Lasting Impressions
My Husband My Love
Never Ever Give Up
The Passion of Chocolate
Peace Be With You
The Perfect Brew
The Power of Inspiration
Sharing the Season
Teddy Bears
There's No Place Like Home

Paperbacks

301 Ways to Stay Young
ABC's of Parenting
Angel-grams
African American Wisdom
Astrology for Cats
Astrology for Dogs
The Be-Attitudes
Birthday Astrologer
Can We Talk
Chocoholic Reasonettes
Cornerstones of Success
Daddy & Me
Erasing My Sanity
Graduation is Just the Beginning
Grandma I Love You
Happiness is Found Along the Way
Hooked on Golf
Ignorance is Bliss
In Celebration of Women
Inspirations
Interior Design for Idiots

Great Quotations, Inc.
1967 Quincy Court
Glendale Heights,IL 60139 USA
Phone: 630-582-2800   Fax: 630-582-2813
http://www.greatquotations.com

Other Titles by Great Quotations, Inc.

Paperbacks

I'm Not Over the Hill
Life's Lessons
Looking for Mr. Right
Midwest Wisdom
Mommy & Me
Mother, I Love You
The Mother Load
Motivating Quotes
Mrs.Murphy's Laws
Mrs. Webster's Dictionary
Only A Sister
The Other Species
Parenting 101
Pink Power
Romantic Rhapsody
The Secret Langauge of Men
The Secret Langauge of Women
The Secrets in Your Name
A Servant's Heart
Social Disgraces
Stress or Sanity
A Teacher is Better Than
Teenage of Insanity
Touch of Friendship
Wedding Wonders
Words From the Coach

Perpetual Calendars

365 Reasons to Eat Chocolate
Always Remember Who Loves You
Best Friends
Coffee Breaks
The Dog Ate My Car Keys
Extraordinary Women
Foundations of Leadership
Generations
The Heart That Loves
The Honey Jar
I Think My Teacher Sleeps at School
I'm a Little Stressed
Keys to Success
Kid Stuff
Never Never Give Up
Older Than Dirt
Secrets of a Successful Mom
Shopoholic
Sweet Dreams
Teacher Zone
Tee Times
A Touch of Kindness
Apple a Day
Golf Forever
Quotes From Great Women
Teacher Are First Class